The Ba...
Wimbledon
AD568

Rupert Matthews

Acknowledgements

Photos, illustrations and maps are by the author except:
statue of Athelbert, Saforrest : River Wandle, Neil Clifton : Wimbledon Hll Road, Ian
Howard : South Wimbledon Tube Station, Chris McKenna (Thryduulf) : Wimbledon
High Street, David Howard
Drawings by Leanne Goodall and Darren Bennett.

Website - www.BretwaldaBooks.com
Twitter - @Bretwaldabooks
Facebook - Bretwalda Books
Blog - bretwaldabooks.blogspot.co.uk/

Bretwalda Books
Unit 8, Fir Tree Close, Epsom,
Surrey KT17 3LD
info@BretwaldaBooks.com
www.BretwaldaBooks.com
ISBN 978-1-909099-65-4

CONTENTS

INTRODUCTION

Wimbledon is now a bustling suburb of south London famous for its tennis tournament, shopping streets, theatre and railway station. But it was not always like that. Some 1500 years ago this was a quiet rural backwater that suddenly was thrown into the limelight of history by a savage battle that was fought here in about the year 568.

As with almost everything about the Age of Arthur, the details are blurred by the passage of time and the lack of contemporary record keeping. Controversies abound and historians argue endlessly over what happened at Wimbledon, when it happened and why it happened. What cannot be denied, however, is that the battle fought here was of prime importance. What was at stake was nothing less than the entire future of southern Britain.

The rulers - Ceawlin and Athelbert - may have been fighting for control of London or the overlordship of neighbouring states, but in retrospect we can see that this battle took place at a crucial juncture. Arthur was dead by this date. The last vestiges of post-Roman Britain were foundering amid economic collapse, cultural decline and military weakness, but the incoming English were as yet a cowed and weakened force.

This was as much a war between nations, cultures and civilisations as it was between rival rulers. What happened here really mattered. Would Britain remain a post-Roman state or would it succumb to barbarian invaders?

Most of the battlefield has now been heavily built over, but the key features can still be picked out: The ford over the Wandle is now Merton High Street. The hillock where Ceawlin first saw his enemy is now occupied by South Wimbledon tube station, the fortress where Ceawlin stood at bay is now Caesar's Camp. And of course Wimbledon Village High Street stands now where it stood then.

The Battle of Wimbledon was a key battle in the Age of Arthur. The future of Britain was at stake. And it all happened right here.

Opposite: Wimbledon High Street as it is today.

CHAPTER 1
THE AGE OF ARTHUR

The Battle of Wimbledon is something of a mystery. We cannot be certain of either the precise site nor the exact date of the battle. But we do know that it was a landmark battle fought between the two most powerful rulers in Britain for control of the island. The winner of the savage struggle fought here would rule most of Britain for the next 20 years. If much about the battle is obscure, the importance of the result is startlingly clear. Put simply this was one of the most decisive battles fought in 6th century Britain.

What might be termed "The Age of Arthur" is a fairly elastic concept. Depending on which historian you listen to it might cover anything from a 50 year period in the early 6th century to all of the 5th and 6th Centuries. The term does, of course, refer to the famous legendary figure of King Arthur. Some historians may quibble on details, but this phrase is a useful term to use when referring to British history between the year 410 when the Roman Empire abandoned Britain through to around 560 when events in the British Isles again began to be recorded in writing.

The Battle of Wimbledon fell toward the end of this period, at a time when historians can agree on some things, but while most remains still obscure.

Almost no contemporary written documents have survived from the Age of Arthur. The historian is reliant on documents written much later or hundreds of miles away. While archaeology can add something to the broad outline of trends, it has little to say about precise events.

Any account of these years must be filled with words such as 'perhaps', 'maybe' and 'probably'. This account of the great battle fought at Wimbledon is no exception, but the broad thrust of events that brought thousands of men to battle to decide the fate of Britain are clear.

When the Roman Emperor Honorius abandoned Britain in 410 - being somewhat preoccupied with the Goths camped outside Rome at the time - he told the locals to look after themselves until Rome had sorted out the barbarians. Once

6

that was achieved the Romans would be back to run Britain again. Of course that never happened. Rome itself fell to the Goths later in 410, then in 476 the last Roman Emperor was deposed by the German King of Italy.

In Britain the Romano-Britons tried to keep their state and civilisation going, with very mixed results. Roman Britain had been ruled by a governor appointed by the Emperor and defended by an army and navy commanded by men similarly appointed from Rome. Local government was in the hands of a dozen or so local councils, the civitates, elected by the richer men in the area.

The sources are not entirely clear, but it would seem that at first the heads of the civitates got together to elect a Governor and military commanders. The first

A Victorian view of the departure of the Romans from Britain in 410. In fact the bulk of the Roman army had left some years earlier, to be replaced by locally raised militias. The events of 410 were more in the way of a breaking of administrative and financial support than a military evacuation.

7

of these elected governors is known to history as Vortigern, though this seems to have been a nickname meaning "wide ruler" or, more informally, "big boss". His real name may have been Vitalinus, a rich man from Gloucester related to the Bishop of London. Certainly his descendants would become great landowners and important nobles in the Severn Valley. Vortigern died about the year 450.

It was during Vortigern's rule that one of the few fixed points in the history of the Age of Arthur has been fixed. We know that at some point during the mid-5th century the government of Britain sent a message to the Roman commander in Gaul and Spain asking for help against the barbarians attacking Britain. The letter

The "Groans of the Britons" was an event that took place about the year 447. Messengers from Britain brought a letter begging the Roman commander in Gaul, Aetius, for help against the barbarians. Aetius could not spare any men, but instead a retired general was sent to offer the Britons advice on self defence.

8

A romanticised 19th century view of the final combat between Arthur and the treacherous Mordred which would end with the deaths of both men. It seems clear that the real Arthur was killed in a civil war with other Romano-Britons.

was addressed to Flavius Aetius "thrice Consul". This allows the letter to be dated to between 446 when Aetius was Consul for the third time and 454 when he was Consul for the fourth time.

The letter is generally known as "The Groans of the Britons" and read, in part, the barbarians drive us to the sea, the sea drives us to the barbarians, between these two means of death we are either killed or drowned."

9

Aetius was too busy with his own wars to send any soldiers to Britain. Instead Britain received a visit from a retired general turned bishop, Germanus of Auxerre. The record of his visit states that he arrived at a south cost port, probably Southampton from the description, where he was warmly welcomed by Roman noblemen. These men would probably have included the ancestors of Ceawlin who fought at Wimbledon. After offering assorted military advice, visiting the shrine of St Albans and making speeches opposing an heretical teaching known as Pelagianism that was gaining ground in Britain, Germanus went home to Gaul.

Vortigern was followed as Governor of post-Roman Britain by a nobleman named Ambrosius Aurelianus. This Aurelianus is recorded as having been a Christian, probably from southern Britain somewhere, perhaps the middle Thames valley, who had noble Roman ancestors. By the time of Ambrosius precise dates

An English raider treads warily as he investigates an abandoned Roman villa. The Saxons, Angles and Jutes who came to settle in Britain during the 5th and 6th centuries would take over political control of much of the island and so found the English nation.

are becoming very difficult to pin down, but he may have died around 470 or 480.

Ambrosius was followed as ruler of what had been Roman Britain by a man named Uther, who took the nickname of Pendragon. The name means "Chief Dragon", and probably refers to the fact that late Roman, and presumably post-Roman, military commanders carried a standard in the shape of a dragon. By extension successful commanders were called "dragons", so "Chief Dragon" would have designated Uther as the supreme military commander of what had been Roman Britain.

At some date, Uther was followed by the famous Arthur. Sometime between 490 and 510 Arthur won the great battle of Badon Hill. This battle saw him lead a united army of Romano-Britons against a large army of invading Saxons, though given the loose terminology of early documents these "Saxons" may have been Angles, Jutes or any other sort of Germanic invader. Arthur's great victory of Badon Hill was followed by several years of peace and relative order in Britain. Somewhere around 530 or 540 Arthur was killed at the Battle of Camlann.

This account would make it seem that post-Roman Britain was a relatively stable and prosperous place, but that was very far from the truth. While the office of Governor survived in some form or other, the underlying institutions and organisation of Roman Britain was collapsing.

At the same time there was a dramatic collapse in the economy and culture of Britain. Trade with the rest of the Roman Empire had brought wealth and prosperity to Britain, but with the Roman Empire imploding that trade died off. Poverty and often starvation stalked the land. The big Roman villas and many towns were abandoned by about 450 as Britain slid from being a wealthy society based on trade and industry to one of subsidence agriculture. The population was in decline, perhaps by as much as half by the year 500. Large areas of what had been productive farmland returned to woodland. This was not a good time to live in Britain.

A disrupting influence to this gradual disintegration of Britain-wide government came from across the North Sea. Both the central government and many of the eastern civitates hired groups of Germanic mercenaries to guard their borders, or to force increasingly reluctant and impoverished farmers to pay their taxes. Many warriors brought their families with them to settle in Britain.

The chronology and course of events is difficult to follow, but while the Romano-Britons sought to retain their culture, power and Christian religion in

11

Britain under rulers such as Vortigern, Ambrosius, Uther and Arthur, the incoming Saxons and Angles eyed the wealth of Britain with covetous eyes. Some of the nascent English took their pay as mercenaries, but others were after bigger prizes. At some date, perhaps as early as the 480s, the English got control of the civitas of Cantium, renaming it Kent. The civitas of the Regni was also taken over by English rulers, the new state later being named Sussex.

By the 560s the majority of Britain remained in the hands of Romano-British rulers. Their society was falling to pieces about them, but they remained in political control. How many civitates retained a Roman-style limited democracy and how many had fallen into the hands of military hard men we do not know. Too many records were lost in the years of chaos that followed for us to be certain. We can be fairly certain, however, that the civitates were by this date largely self-governing. They did still recognize the vague and indeterminate over lordship of the man who occupied the office descended from that of the Roman governor.

The death of Arthur has traditionally been seen as marking the effective end of the Governor as a position of any real power . Historians have tended to see Arthur's death as being a major opportunity for the nascent English. After all it was Arthur who had defeated them at Badon Hill and these English would later conquer most of Britain. But that was not how things seemed at the time.

All the earliest sources agree that Arthur was killed during a civil war fought between Romano-Britons in which the English took no part. Mordred, the man responsible for Arthur's death, was also killed at Camlann. Mordred seems to have come from northern Britain, but not much else is known about him. What is clear is that whatever power the men claiming the position of Governor still exercised largely vanished. The immediate winners were the men who ruled the civitates. Each of these petty states became effectively independent.

The title of Pendragon was at about this point taken by Maelgwn, ruler of Gwynedd in what is now north Wales. What power he wielded as Pendragon is quite unknown, but his contemporary Gildas wrote of him in disparaging terms saying he was unfit to hold the title. After Maelgwn's death his son Rhun Hir (the Tall) took over Gwynedd and tried to enforce his claim to the overlordship of Britain south of Hadrian's Wall. He was successful only north of the midlands, southern Britain was up for grabs and two monarchs seem to have made the try. It was these two men who would fight each other at Wimbledon.

CHAPTER 2
COMMANDERS AT WIMBLEDON

The Battle of Wimbledon was fought between two very different men leading very different armies. The first of these was Ceawlin. Later generations would remember Ceawlin as an early ruler of the Kingdom of Wessex, but he himself would have seen himself as a Prince of the Belgae. This civitas covered what is now Hampshire and Wiltshire and at some point had taken over the civitas of the Durotriges, modern Dorset. The Belgae had recently lost a war, and with it much of what is now Somerset, to the civitas of the Dobunni, which covered what is now Gloucestershire, Worcestershire and much of the Severn Valley. The failure of Rhun Hir to take over as overlord of Britain will have been seen by Ceawlin as an opportunity.

For a man of these times we know quite a lot about Ceawlin. Or to be more accurate we know what a monk writing about him a hundred or so years later thought to have been the truth. According to this later account, Ceawlin was a son of Cynric the ruler of the civitas of the Belgae from about 534 to 560. Ceawlin was brought up to follow his father as the ruler of a Christian, Romano-British state - albeit one that was greatly impoverished and seriously lacking in sophisticated culture. He is recorded to have been in Southampton as a young warrior greeting clergymen visiting from France in around 550.

Probably when he was in his teens, Ceawlin was sent to the great monastery of Glastonbury to be educated. Certainly he was a Christian, and it would seem a reasonably devout one. The monks of Glastonbury invited Ceawlin to remain as their abbot, and this has been interpreted to indicate that the young prince was exceptionally devout and learned. In fact it may simply have been that the monks thought it would do their abbey good to have a royal as abbot. In any case, Ceawlin's father wrote a letter telling Ceawlin to come home and take up his duties as a leader of his people.

According to the Anglo-Saxon Chronicle, Ceawlin fought his first battle in 556 at "Beran Byrg". The year may be as unreliable as any in documents of this date,

13

but the place can be fixed. Beran Byrg is now known as Barbury in Wiltshire. In the 6th century Barbury was a border fortress between the Belgae and the Dobunni. There had been at least one war between the two civitates, and now there was another. Barbury was an impressive fortress surrounded by earth and timber fortification topping precipitous slopes. It had been built in pre-Roman times but was now refortified and garrisoned. The battle would appear to have been caused by an invasion launched by the Dobunni.

There are two relevant facts about this battle. The first is that the Belgae were under the joint command of Cynric and Ceawlin. Presumably the older, experienced Cynric was taking his son on a campaign to learn the trade of warfare. The other feature is that the battle saw Ceawlin fighting a battle at a refurbished hillfort. Throughout his career, Ceawlin would favour such tactical ground. The other recurring feature in his military career was to be battles fought to control a river crossing.

Although the actual dates in these early chronicles are rather unreliable, the chronology is thought to be sound. That the battle at Barbury is said to have been fought in 556 may not be taken literally, but the placing of this battle as being 12 years before the Wimbledon campaign is probably not far off the mark.

What Ceawlin was doing during those ten years or so is nowhere recorded. Presumably he was learning the arts of diplomacy, administration and soldiering that were expected of a post-Roman British leader. He may not have fought any pitched battles in these years, but he must be presumed to have taken part in some campaigns. At some point Cynric died and Ceawlin became ruler of the Belgae. Working with him was a man named Cutha who was either his brother or his uncle, the sources contradict each other.

Ceawlin's age during the Wimbledon campaign is not known for certain. Given the events in his life to date, however, he was probably at least 23.

If Ceawlin was an experienced soldier, his opponent was very much the opposite.

King Athelbert of Kent was at the very start of a career that would prove to be long and impressive, but at this date he was a very young and inexperienced man.

A statue of Athelbert, King of Kent, on the facade of Canterbury Cathedral. In 568 Canterbury was the capital of the English Kingdom of Kent, but the Christian community in this largely pagan kingdom was small. The cathedral would not be founded until more than 30 years after the Battle of Wimbledon.

He may have been only a teenager. The historical sources are inconsistent when it comes to Athelbert's reign with some sources saying he became King of Kent in 560, others 565 and still others 589. These dates need not be entirely inconsistent since it was not unknown for early English kings to have their chosen successor crowned as joint king alongside themselves. Perhaps Athelbert's father Eormenric had him crowned as a joint king in 560 or 565 when the younger man was very young indeed, but did not actually die and hand over power until 589.

At any rate Athelbert was young and inexperienced in 565. He had with him two older men named Oslaf and Cnebba. These men are described as being "Ealdormen", a fairly loose term that indicates that they held their positions directly from the king. What those positions may have been is not stated, but given that they were on a military campaign they were presumably military men as opposed to administrators or tax collectors.

It has been suggested, though this is mere supposition, that Eormenric sent his young son Athelbert to command the Wimbledon campaign as a way for the young man to learn the trade of warfare and win some early glory. Assuming Oslaf and Cnebba were experienced commanders then they may have been sent by Eormenric to keep an eye on the young prince and, perhaps, were the real commanders of the expedition.

At this date Kent was a pagan, English kingdom. The people of Kent wore clothes and used household goods more like those of northern Germany than those of Britain. They spoke a Germanic language and they worshiped deities such as Woden, Freya and Thunor. Until the death of Maelgwn they seem to have recognised the vague overlordship of the line of post-Roman governors, but they had never really been part of the post-Roman British culture. Certainly at this date they had close ties to the powerful Germanic Kingdom of the Franks that was uniting the fractured remains of Roman Gaul into early-modern France.

Kent may have been a small kingdom, but it had powerful backing from the Franks, access to large numbers of mercenaries from Germany and seems to have been bursting with a restive energy. Like Ceawlin, Athelbert will have seen the failure of Rhun as a chance to hit the big time.

It was not just ambition that pitted Ceawlin and Athelbert against each other. There was also money and trade to fight over. Although the cross-Channel trade was much reduced by this date, what was left was still valuable. Moreover, rulers at this time found it easy to tax goods going in or out of ports so controlling trade was disproportionately important to a ruler.

In the past both Kent and the Belgae had been important maritime states. Kent had traded across the narrow straits from their big port at Dubris (Dover) while the Belgae had used the port at Clausentum (Southampton). Both states had also fielded warships and while the evidence for such craft at this date is lacking it would be reasonable to assume that both retained some form of naval power.

We do not know exactly what it was that sparked the war between Ceawlin and Athelbert, but the campaign when it began was fought on land, not at sea.

Southern Britain at about the time of the Battle of Wimbledon. At this date only Kent and Sussex are known to have been under English rule, with most of the other civitates remaining under the political control of the local Romano-British nobility. All borders are approximate.

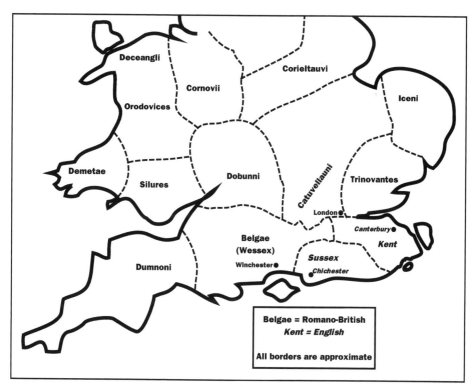

17

CHAPTER 3
THE MARCH TO WIMBLEDON

Whatever the cause of the war, both rulers seem to have been keen to get to grips with each other as quickly as possible. A problem for them both was how to get at each other. The Kingdom of the South Saxons covered what is now Sussex, blocking a direct route from Ceawlin's capital at Venta (now Winchester) and Athelbert's at Cantwareburh (now Canterbury). We do not know who was King of Sussex at this date. Cissa had died in about 550 and the names of his successors were lost when the kingdom ceased to be an independent state some two centuries later.

In any case the dense forests that then covered the Weald and the heavy clay soils on which they stood made for hard travelling. The Romans had built several roads running south from London to connect with iron ore mines and smelting workshops in the Weald, and one branch turned west to Winchester but none went east to Kent.

Effectively the belligerents had two choices. They could either march along the route on the North Downs that is now known as the Pilgrim's Way or they could use the Roman roads that led from their respective states to London.

At this date London was a shadow of its former self, and tiny in relation to what it would become, but was still a place of importance. We know that numerous workshops, houses and warehouses lined the river upstream of the old Roman city. The beach here was ideal for the small ships of the day to be moored so that at low tide they were stranded and could be unloaded easily. The road along which these buildings stood is still called The Strand. How the old Roman City was being used is unclear, but its city walls still stood and could be easily defended.

London was a prosperous and, by the standards of the time, a wealthy place. The taxes raised from the London merchants would have been enough to make any ruler rich. It is not known which state ruled it at this time, so it may be that it was for control of London that the war was fought. So the rival rulers would

18

both have marched for London as quickly as possible, if for no other reason than to take advantage

Athelbert's route would have been simple. He could march his army straight up the Roman road that ran straight as an arrow from Canterbury to London. This road was later known as Watling Street, and later still as the A2.

Ceawlin's options were more complex as there was no direct Roman road on

The surroundings of Wimbledon in about 565. The old Roman road of Stane Street was the main route to London from the southwest. Kingston, as the first crossing place over the Thames upstream of London, was a commercial centre of growing importance. Wimbledon was a small village. Ewell was a crumbling Roman posting station which may have been almost uninhabited. London remained a pre-eminent trading centre and the bridge over the Thames seems to have been intact at this date. The River Wandle may have been the boundary between Kent to the east and Belgae to the west.

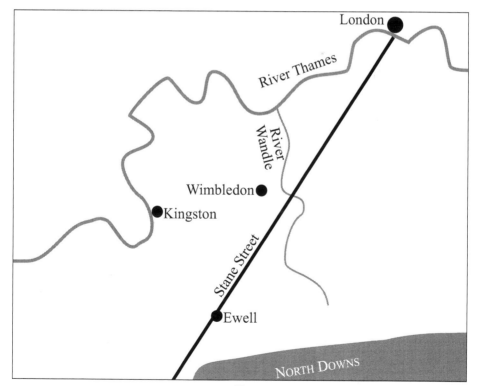

which to march. He could have taken the Roman route east to Noviomagus (Chichester) then north up the Roman road later known as Stane Street. That, however, meant going through Sussex and we have no idea of the attitude of the South Saxons to the war. Another route was to march north to Calleva, now Silchester, then east to Pontes (Staines) to reach London from the west. That route would have had the attraction of taking Ceawlin close to the lands of his allies the Gewisse. These people were a group of Saxon mercenaries and their families settled around Dorchester on Thames. The name means "reliable ones" and was probably the name adopted by these mercenaries as something of a marketing ploy.

However, Ceawlin and Cutha seem to have taken a third route. This was to go east along the Pilgrim's Way to the junction with Stane Street near what is now Epsom. They then turned northeast along Stane Street to London. Given the location of the battle at Wimbledon, it seems most likely that Ceawlin was marching up Stane Street.

Stane Street crossed the River Wandle at what is now Christchurch Road, Merton. Today the area is heavily built up and the Wandle is constrained between concrete banks. Back in 568, however, the river was a considerable obstacle. It would have been much wider than today and its banks lined with trees and marshy ground. An army on the march complete with pack horses or carts carrying supplies could have crossed it only at a ford or bridge. It was for this reason that many Dark Age battles were fought at river crossing points. An army on the defensive could be certain that an invading army would use the river crossing. Moreover the ford was usually narrow, negating the advantage of numbers that a larger army would enjoy.

We cannot be certain what happened here in 568, but it would make sense if Athelbert had got to London first, then marched down Stane Street to block Ceawlin's advance at the ford over the Wandle.

Marching northeast up Stane Street, Ceawlin would have had the presence of Athelbert and his army at the ford reported back to him by his scouts. He may have ridden forward to see the situation for himself, perhaps getting a good view by pausing on the slight hill where South Wimbledon Tube Station now stands. Ceawlin would then have to decide what to do next. In making his decision, Ceawlin would have taken into account the abilities and skills of the men who would be fighting on both sides.

CHAPTER 3
MEN, WEAPONS AND TACTICS

W e do not know either the size or composition of the two armies at Wimbledon in 568, but other sources and archaeology can tell us what types of armies these were.

The English army that had marched from Kent would have been made up almost exclusively of infantry. The men may have ridden on small ponies when on the march or when scouting. There is some evidence that they may have ridden horses when pursuing a defeated enemy, and presumably when trying escape a defeat themselves, but battles were fought on foot.

The training, equipment and tactics of an English army at this date was determined by the way it was recruited. There were two methods of recruitment. First each king and nobleman had what was known as his "hird", a word that means "hearth" but which is usually translated as "hearth troop" or "bodyguard". These were men who lived in his hall, sat around his hearth at night and were maintained at his expense. These men were professional warriors who had no duties other than to fight for their lord, and to train constantly for that purpose.

These men were rewarded with food, drink and games. If they performed a job well they were given gifts of ostentatious luxury - an armring of silver or gold would be typical. They were used by a lord for a variety of purposes in addition to actual fighting. They would escort him on journeys to emphasise his status, they would enforce order, pursue and capture criminals and generally act as the muscle behind a lord's right to rule.

The bodyguard of a king or noble were expected to protect him to the death. So long as their leader stayed on the battlefield, they had to stay as well. When or if he retreated they had to protect his escape. If he were killed they had to protect his body and get it away for decent burial. If this were not possible they had to stay and die with him - surrender was not an option.

The next body of men Athelbert could call on were his thegns, literally "men who serve". These were men granted lands on which to live. The grander thegns

An English nobleman. His armour and equipment is based on that of the man buried in the Sutton Hoo ship burial. The helmet is of iron decorated with embossed silver panels, some of which are gilded. The inside of the helmet is lined with leather, padded with wool. The mail shirt reaches to the elbows and knees, and is held in place at the waist by belt that helps to take some of the weight off the shoulders. The links of the mail are of iron. Some men had gold or silver links inserted to form a pattern within the mail. The shield is of lime wood with a leather cover. The rim of the shield is covered with iron, and iron straps extend from the rim to the boss. He carries a pointed, double-edged sword as his main weapon. The hilt of the sword would have been wrapped with leather, while the pommel would have been of solid gold, inlaid with garnets or similar semi-precious stones. The scabbard of the sword would have been similarly embellished with gold, silver and stones. The belt is of leather studded with gold or silver ornaments and fastened by a buckle of solid gold. Going to war for the English was as much about intimidating the enemy with a show of wealth and confidence as about fighting.

had estates large enough that they did not need to work them personally, but took a share of the produce made by those who did. Further down the scale were thegns who worked the land themselves. These men owed service to the king in the form of military service. They were not full time professionals like the hird, but they were expected to come fully armed and reasonably well trained. They also had to bring with them bacon, biscuits and other food to last them for the campaign - plus presumably a servant or horse to carry it.

In theory the entire male population was obliged to turn out armed and ready to fight, but this "fyrd" as it was known, seems to have been only for local defence and would not have gone on a prolonged campaign.

Because the bulk of an English army was made up of part time soldiers, it was generally not capable of sophisticated tactics or subtle manoeuvres. The basic military formation of the English was the shield wall. This involved the men being drawn up shoulder to shoulder so that their shields overlapped and presented a solid wall to the enemy. Several ranks of men were arranged in this way, standing closely behind each other. Generally the resulting formation was as wide as it

An English warrior. This man is based on the standard equipment of a Kentish warrior of the middling class at about this time. He wears the standard clothing of a woollen or linen tunic to his knees with tight sleeves. The legs are covered by trousers over which are wound puttee-like strips of cloth or leather. His shoes are of leather. Over the tunic he wears a leather jacket that reaches to elbows and waist. On his head is a helmet made of toughened leather. These helmets might be strengthened with a metal crest or rim. The shield is made of lime wood over which has been stretched a leather covering. The rim of the shield is strengthened with iron. It is held by a central hand hold hidden behind the iron boss. His main weapon is a spear about eight feet long. The shaft is of ash wood and the tip of steel. His sword is for use if the spear breaks.

23

needed to be to block a river crossing or line a hilltop and as deep as the numbers of men present allowed. It is thought that the best equipped men were at the front, and the older men at the back. This was not so much because older men were weaker than that they were more experienced in battle. The older men were tasked with shifting resources from one part of the line to another as required. The king, or other leader, usually stood in the centre of the formation with his personal bodyguard of heavily armoured men, all grouped under the main battle standard.

The basic equipment of an English warrior at this date was the spear and the shield. Spears were about seven feet long with an iron blade of about 10 inches or so at the business end. The shaft was made of ash, or another close-grained wood that could withstand shocks and thrusts easily. Shields were almost universally circular and about three feet in diameter. The body of the shields was mostly of lime wood as this timber retained the sap and remained 'sticky' for some time after being felled. It would thus grip any arrows or javelins that came its way. The shields were faced with cow hides that were first boiled to become supple, then stretched over the wood and nailed in place to shrink and harden. Some shields were edged with metal bands for extra strength.

Most men also carried a side arm of some kind in case the spear broke - usually a large knife with a heavy, single edged blade known as a scramasax. Other men had a dagger or a small axe. Many men also carried two or three light javelins. A few men, but not many, carried a bow and arrows to war. Only wealthy men could afford a sword.

Armour of any kind was expensive and rare at this date. Only richer men could expect to go into battle with the advantage of armour. The most numerous pieces of armour at this date among the English were a shirt of chain mail that reached to the elbows and to mid-thigh. Helmets were of a simple conical shape, with more elaborate examples having flaps hanging down over the neck, cheeks and sometimes over the eyes. Less wealthy men might have had breastplates and helmets made of toughened leather, but it is not clear how widespread this sort of equipment was.

Kings and nobles wore armour of quite exceptional quality and gaudiness. It was not at all unusual for helmets and shields to be covered in gold leaf, decorated with embossed silver plaques or set with garnets, amber or other semi-precious stones. Weapons were also richly decorated with silver, gold and stones.

Most battles began with the leaders meeting to talk. This might be to seek a peaceful solution, but most leaders used it as a way to intimidate and assess the

An English force drawn up in the shieldwall ready for combat. Each man stands shoulder to shoulder with the man next to him, while the formation is eight men deep. This seems to have been a common depth for a shieldwall, but the formation could be thinner or thicker depending on the width of space to be defended and the men available. When the enemy approached the shields were held in front of the men, with each shield overlapping that of its neighbour to the left by a foot or so. In this way a solid barrier, or wall, or shields was presented to the enemy. The spears were usually held overhead to thrust over the shields and down at the enemy. Swords or scramaseax could be used to thrust over or under the shields. Only the front two ranks could use their weapons. The men behind would step forward to replace casualties or would push and heave as if in a vicious rugby scrum to try to build forward momentum.

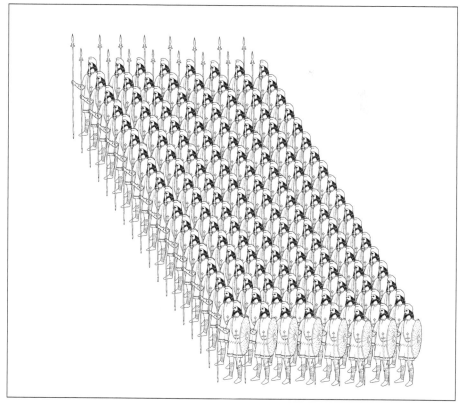

This figure of a Romano-British cavalryman is based on written descriptions from Gaul, supported by archaeological evidence from Britain. He is mounted on a fairly small, but sturdy horse. His saddle is of leather, but he lacks stirrups as they had not yet reached Europe. He wears woollen trousers of a checked pattern and a woollen tunic. Over these he wars a coat of mail, backed by leather. The belt around his waist is of leather, hidden behind a sash of silk or linen. The colouring of these sashes may have indicated rank. On his head he wears an iron helmet lined with leather and padded with wool. The crest on the helmet is of horsehair and in all written sources is said to have been dyed yellow. The shield is of wood faced with leather but apparently not strengthened with iron edges. It is oval in shape, about two feet wide and three feet tall. He holds only one javelin, having presumably already thrown the other two at the enemy. His fairly short sword is suspended from his leather belt. The cloak is of wool and could be of almost any colour. There are hints that the colour of the cloak indicated to which unit the soldier belonged.

This post-Roman soldier is based on a soldier shown in a 6th century mosaic in Italy. He is equipped as a heavy infantry man who would have fought in the main battle formation. His medium-sized wooden shield is painted with the Christian Chi-Rho symbol in blue and white on a green background. The shield boss is painted in six separate coloured sections. He wears a red tunic over white trousers. The hem of the tunic and shoulders are covered with yellow cloth, which may have been distinctive for his unit. His thrusting spear is about six feet long and in the mosaic appears to be his main weapon, but we know from written sources that these men carried a sword. He wears no armour at all. The necklace around his neck is of gold in the mosaic, which might mark him out as being an officer of some kind. He is probably indicative of the men of the militia recruited by the civitates of Britain.

enemy. By getting close to the enemy army, an experienced commander could study it for weak spots, gauge the equipment and morale of the men and thus formulate a plan of attack.

Insults were a favoured way of seeking to undermine enemy morale. This was not merely a matter of telling the enemy commander he was ugly, but was a highly skilled art. A pre-battle insult was expected to display a close knowledge of gossip and facts about the opponent, his family, his eating habits and sexual proclivities. And the insults were ideally to be delivered in verse that not only rhymed but alliterated as well. A really good insult would be remembered for years to come.

Such formalities over, the favoured English battle tactic was to start with attempts to intimidate the enemy. The army would sing, chant and wave their weapons and banners. Individuals might push their way out in front of the army to juggle with weapons or shout insulting poems at the enemy. Once the commander felt his men had achieved as much as they could, he would order the

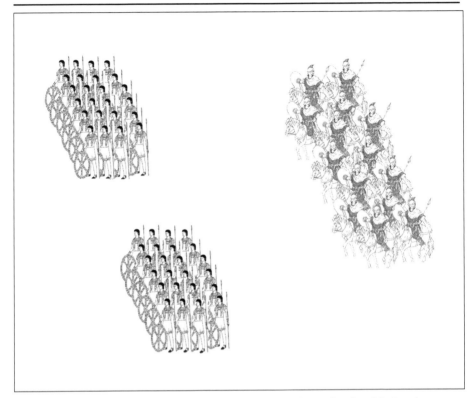

Written sources indicate that post-Roman states adopted a flexible battle formation that called for a high degree of training. The militia infantry were drawn up in small units separated by gaps. This allowed them to manoeuvre more easily about the battlefield. Behind them were positioned the cavalry ready to move forward to skirmish by throwing javelins or to charge home as the occasion demanded. Such tactical sophistication was beyond the skills of the majority of barbarians these armies faced.

advance. When the army got close enough to the enemy they would unleash a shower of arrows and javelins. This would, it was hoped, not only inflict casualties but also disrupt the enemy formation.

The men would then charge the enemy using their own shield wall in an effort to smash a way through that of the enemy. This rarely happened, so the battle would then settle down to a period of savage butchery. Those in the front two or three ranks would seek to stab forward with their spears to kill enemy warriors, while using their shields to protect themselves. The rear ranks would push and heave, shoving forwards to drive the enemy line back. A warrior stepping backwards was more likely to trip and fall, becoming more vulnerable to a spear thrust. A clever commander might have positioned somewhere along his line a team of especially tough, strong warriors who at a given signal would pile forwards to punch a narrow wedge into the enemy line. If that gap could be widened and exploited the enemy formation might be broken.

Once the enemy shield wall was broken open it would be easier for the advancing army to kill their adversaries. Most casualties occurred at this stage of the battle.

Quite how many men Athelbert took with him to Wimbledon is unknown. We know that on other occasions, the Kingdom of Kent could put 5,000 men into the field but this seems to have been exceptional. Perhaps Athelbert had 2,000 men with him in 568.

Ceawlin's army is more difficult to reconstruct with accuracy. Our sources for the Romano-Britons are less detailed and mostly fragmentary. However, enough remains for us to be reasonably certain that armies such as that of the Belgae were similar in organisation and deployment to those of the post-Roman states in Gaul, Spain and other western provinces.

A post-Roman civitas would have fielded an army of mixed infantry and cavalry. As with the English the way in which the men were recruited had a huge influence on how they fought.

The civitates had, since at least the 370s, been raising militia from among their own citizens. These militia seem to have been full time employees of the state and while they were equipped as were contemporary Roman soldiers, their duties seem to have included what we might consider police action as much as fighting wars. Moreover they were paid and equipped by the civitas that they served, and so owed their loyalty to the civitas not to the Roman state.

When money and men stopped coming from the Empire in 410, it was these militias that took over the task of protecting Britain from invasion. They continued the tactics and equipment of the late Roman Empire.

The infantry were generally better equipped than their English counterparts with leather armour and helmets being the norm. Swords were more common among such men than among the English, but the combination of heavy thrusting spear and big shield would have been very similar.

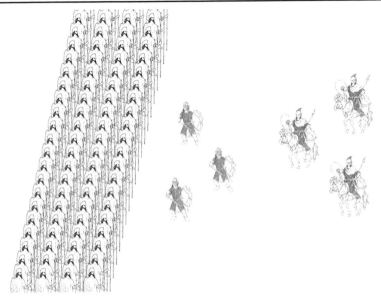

A Romano-British cavalry attack on an English shieldwall. Above: The commanders meet and exchange insults. Below the cavalry move forward to throw javelins and probe for weaknesses.

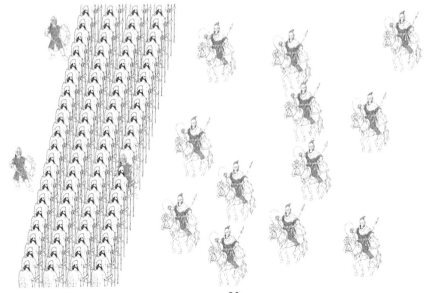

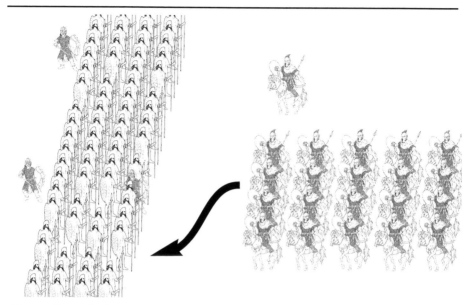

Above: Once the Romano-British commander has identified a weak spot he launches his column to attack. Below: The horsemen push forward, jostling through the shieldwall, breaking it apart and gaining the victory.

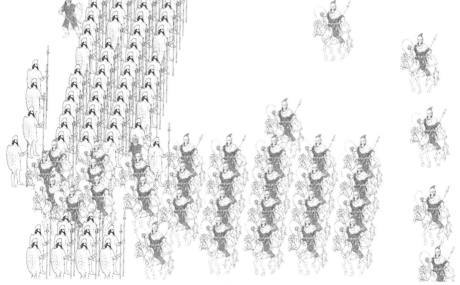

31

They were organised on a decimal basis, with units of 100 men being divided into groups of 10 for the purposes of issuing rations and perhaps for battlefield use as well. We know of several occasions on which the basic units of 100 men were combined in groups of ten to produce a troop of 1,000 men.

Being full time professionals and drawing on the military heritage and training manuals of the Roman Empire, these infantry could perform sophisticated manoeuvres. They seem to have routinely formed up in small square blocks of men that were separated from each other by gaps of open ground. The cavalry were stationed behind or on the flanks of these infantry groups. The small formations of the infantry were much more flexible than those of the English. They could change direction rapidly, form line or column or switch between the two as the occasion demanded.

The main role of these men on the battlefield was to hold ground securely. They acted as a mobile shield around which the cavalry could manoeuvre, charge, fall back, regroup and move with safety.

These cavalry were present in only small numbers, the scanty records we have talk about armies having 60, 180 or 300 such horseman when the infantry were numbered in the thousands. Yet although small in number the horsemen could be highly effective. At the Battle of Clermont-Ferrard in 471 a charge by 18 Romano-Gaul cavalry destroyed a shieldwall of 2,000 Goths.

These cavalry rode horses that would today be considered small and were usually equipped with armour and helmets as well as shields. Because they lacked the stirrup they could not perform the type of charge home with couched lance that would make the medieval knight so awesomely effective. Instead they used tactics that dated back to the time of Alexander the Great.

These men were adept at sweeping, swirling charges that would take them close enough to an enemy to throw their javelins, but would take them back out of range before they could suffer much damage themselves. Each man seems to have been equipped with three or four javelins, and they were highly skilled at their use. Riding at full gallop, these men could throw a javelin up to 100 feet with accuracy. Being on the receiving end of such a barrage, when trying to hit back involved trying to hit a fast moving target that was changing direction.

For closer fighting the cavalry had long, straight swords and shields. On the field of battle such cavalry could be devastating, but their horses took years to train and their equipment was expensive.

The preferred tactic of Romano-British cavalry would be to first engage in a swirling, fast-moving skirmish as they deluged the enemy line with volley after volley of javelins. Their commander would be watching the progress of the assault to determine if the enemy were being disordered or demoralised by the attack. If they were the cavalry would move on to the second phase of the attack, though if not either the attack would be called off or the task left to the infantry.

Because they could not charge home without the very real risk of falling off, the cavalry instead attacked at a trot. The usual formation was a column ordered several ranks deep and sometimes shaped like a wedge with the point to the enemy. The point of impact was chosen carefully with the commander selecting the point in the enemy shieldwall where the opposing formation was disordered or starting to fray.

After a final volley of javelins thrown at very close range, the horsemen drew their swords and got to close quarters. Killing the enemy with the sword was perhaps the most obvious task, but not the most important one. What the

In addition to their militia, apparently recruited from among their own citizens, the civitates employed numbers of Germanic mercenaries. This figure is based on a verbal description of a Frankish mercenary of this date. He wears a fur jerkin over a woollen tunic with distinctively Frankish horizontal stripes of red, blue or yellow. His wooden shield is rather smaller than is usual for Germans. The axe tucked into his leather belt is the famous "francisca", a throwing axe that was able to split open shields and smash through armour. The Franks habitually threw these weapons as they closed with the enemy to disorder opposing ranks and open a path for a charge to punch through. His main weapon is a thrusting spear, though he also carries a short, straight sword that can be seen below his shield.

33

horsemen were really aiming to do was to use the weight and bulk of their horses to jostle and push their way into the enemy formation. Lashing out with their swords would cause the enemy to fall back, while the horses were trained to kick, bite and push against men on foot. Horsemen can be highly intimidating as well as dangerous to those unaccustomed to dealing with them.

As the horsemen pushed deeper into the enemy formation, those behind would be driving their horses forward to add their muscle power and weight to those in front. If momentum could be built up and sustained the drive of horsemen into the infantry shieldwall would become unstoppable. Within a few minutes the leading survivors of the horsemen would be through and out the other side. They would then be free to wheel about and attack the enemy infantry from behind.

Meanwhile the infantry supporting the cavalry would have moved up to close with the front of the enemy shieldwall. Faced by enemies in front and rear, the opposing infantry formation would break and be reduced to a fleeing rabble. They could then be pursued by the horsemen, this time hacking down at helpless fugitives with their swords.

On the face of it the Romano-Britons had a huge advantage over their Germanic enemies. Their men were better equipped, better trained and possessed of superior tactics. In fact it was the English who were in the ascendent. The problem was primarily one of cost.

The Romano-British system had been developed for a prosperous Roman Empire with a cash economy, effective tax collection system and sophisticated bureaucracy. But by the mid-6th century none of those things survived. The Romano-British states were in decline as a cooling climate reduced crop harvests and falling populations reduced manpower.

Well-trained, full time soldiers were expensive things. It was much cheaper to hire mercenaries, so the Romano-Britons were hiring increasingly large numbers of Germanic warriors to do their fighting for them. Ceawlin had the Gewisse, but other states had their mercenary troops. Increasingly these men, fighting as did their opponents, replaced the Romano-British infantry. The sophisticated infantry tactics became a thing of the past to be replaced by shieldwalls. The Romano-British cavalry remained as skilled as ever, but without the infantry support that they were used to they lost some of their effectiveness.

We have no way of knowing how far this process had gone by the time of the Battle of Wimbledon, but it would prove to be ultimately fatal to the survival of the Romano-British states themselves.

Chapter 5
The Battle of Wimbledon

The course of the Battle of Wimbledon is not recorded in any detail in any of the near contemporary sources. However, it is possible to deduce a possible course of events from the few details that are known and by comparing it to other battles fought by Ceawlin.

We can assume that the day of battle opened with Athelbert's army blocking the ford over the Wandle at Merton. This was, and would remain, a favoured tactic of the English. Battles around fords were common as a defending commander would know that an advancing enemy had to use the ford, and so could be certain of meeting his opponent there. Fords could also be easy to defend as the frontage on which an enemy could advance was limited. Given that Athelbert would have been wary of Ceawlin's strength in cavalry, defending a ford would be a sound tactic. It would force Ceawlin to advance with his infantry and thus put them on a level footing with the Kentish army.

Ceawlin and his army, meanwhile, would have been marching northeast along Stane Street. The battle was named after Wibba's Hill, yet the land around here is generally flat. The only real hill lies two miles to the west, and that is a poor thing rising some 60 feet above the Wandle. The hill is now occupied by Wimbledon village, the old heart of Wimbledon, so it must be assumed that this was the place known in 568 as Wibba's Hill. Perhaps the eponymous Wibba had a farm here. North and west of Wimbledon Village stretches Wimbledon Common.

The main fighting would therefore take place some distance from the ford and from Stane Street. This was due to one of the most noticeable features on the hill. Near the western end of the hill where the slope looks down to the Coombe brook with Kingston Hill beyond there is an ancient earthwork that is today known as Caesar's Camp. The ring of earthworks had nothing to do with Caesar, nor with any Roman, it was built around

35

300BC by the Celts. The earthworks today are insignificant, having been levelled in the 19th century by a property developer, but originally they would have formed a formidable obstacle. The ditch was about 10 feet deep and the bank on the inside as high again. The circular earthwork is about 300 yards across and now lies on a golf course.

The conventional view is that in 568 the earthwork had been abandoned for some centuries, but that view is now being questioned. The effective destruction of the earthworks in 1865 not only levelled the ditch and rampart but also removed any archaeological evidence of what had once been here. In particular it destroyed evidence to indicate whether or not the fortress had been refortified during the Age of Arthur.

We know that many of these old, pre-Roman forts were reused in the post-Roman age. Some were completely rebuilt with stone and timber

The River Wandle to the south of Wimbledon at Beddington. In 568 the river would have been wider and more overgrown than it is today, representing a significant obstacle to travellers, hence the importance of the ford.

South Wimbledon tube station. Although not easy to make out given the built up nature of the surroundings today, this tube station stands on a slight rise beside what was Stane Street. It would have been from this spot that a man advancing up Stane Street from the southwest would first have seen the ford over the River Wandle. Presumably Ceawlin's scouts, and perhaps Ceawlin himself, studied the Kent army from near this spot.

walls, elaborate gate towers and extensive interior buildings, indicating a ruler had paid for the work. Others were patched up with a small palisade and contained only a few huts, perhaps having been occupied by a farmer and his livestock.

The fort at Wimbledon overlooked a Roman road at a key crossing point

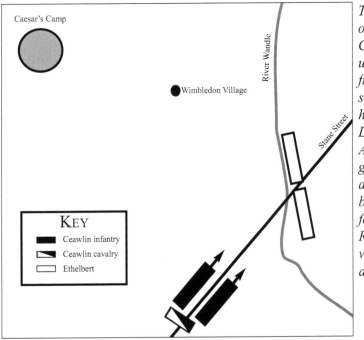

The battle opened with Ceawlin coming up Stane Street from the southwest heading toward London. Athelbert had got there first and was blocking the ford over the River Wandle with his Kentish army.

Having studied the Kent army defending the ford, Ceawlin leads his army to Caesar's Camp to adopt a defensive position. Seeing the move, the Kent army crosses the ford and pursues.

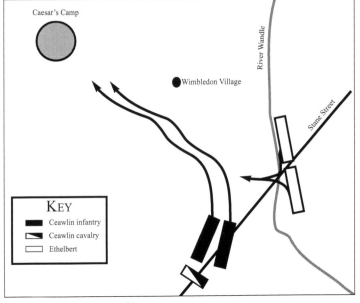

over a river and stood close to the borders between three powerful states: Kent, Belgae and Catuvellauni. It would have been surprising had it not been given a garrison of some kind to keep an eye on who used the road, and to extract customs and tribute payments. It must be presumed that the fort had been refortified to some extent.

We know that Ceawlin fought at least three other battles at similarly restored ancient earthworks - at Barbury in Wiltshire in 556, at Dyrham in Somerset in 577 and at Alton Priors, again in Wiltshire, in 592. There was clearly something about these old earthworks that suited Ceawlin and his way of doing battle. What that was is uncertain, but some early sources indicate that Arthur himself had deployed a battle plan that involved a

A view looking northwest up Wimbledon Hill Road from Wimbledon Railway Station. This was all open country at the time of the battle. Ceawlin's army marched up this route as they headed toward's Caesar's Camp on what is now Wimbledon Common.

hillfort with devastating consequences at his great victory over the English at Badon Hill.

The early sources make two definite statements about Badon Hill. First they say that it was a siege, as opposed to a battle or skirmish, that lasted for three days. Second they record that the victory was gained by a charge led by Arthur himself in which 960 Englishmen were killed. It is not too difficult to reconstruct what these statements mean.

It would seem that Arthur had retreated back inside the fortifications and had allowed the infantry English to wear themselves out attacking the defences. Once the English were depleted or disordered, Arthur had sallied out with his cavalry to launch a charge that smashed the English shieldwall and drove them off in rout with heavy losses. It would be reasonable to assume that Ceawlin adopted a similar tactic at Wimbledon.

If this were the case, then Ceawlin would not have attempted to force the ford at Merton, but instead would have turned his army aside and marched north to Caesar's Camp on the hill to the north. There he would have placed his horsemen out of harm's way while the militia infantry and Gewisse mercenaries manned the defences.

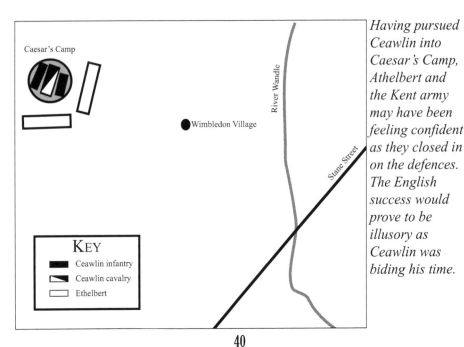

Having pursued Ceawlin into Caesar's Camp, Athelbert and the Kent army may have been feeling confident as they closed in on the defences. The English success would prove to be illusory as Ceawlin was biding his time.

Caesar's Camp

River Wandle

Wimbledon Village

Stane Street

KEY
Ceawlin infantry
Ceawlin cavalry
Ethelbert

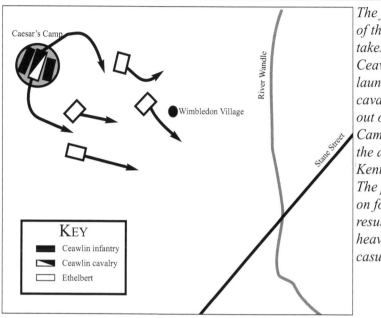

The final stage of the battle takes place as Ceawlin launches a cavalry charge out of Caesar's Camp to attack the dispersed Kentish infantry. The pursuit went on for hours and resulted in heavy Kentish casualties.

That left Athelbert with a decision to make. He could stay where he was, retreat or attack. He had not come all this way merely to retreat without a blow struck, and standing on the ford was clearly getting him nowhere. He must have decided to follow Ceawlin to the earthworks for the fighting took place there. Presumably he thought that Ceawlin was on the run and that an attack on a defended position was a job for infantry. And so he led his infantry forwards.

If Athelbert thought he had Ceawlin trapped, he was wrong. In fact this was what Ceawlin had wanted. He had laid a trap and Athelbert had walked into it. The attack by the Kentish men failed, but Ceawlin's plan worked.

The English assault on the ramparts was held, after which Ceawlin launched his cavalry. We know that two important Englishmen noblemen were killed here. These were Oslaf and Cnebba, the experienced men who may have been set to keep an eye on young Athelbert. We also know that once the army of Kent had been pushed back the retreat became a rout. Ceawlin and his men chased them all the way back to Kent. Athelbert himself got away, but many of his men did not.

41

CHAPTER 5
AFTERMATH

The Battle of Wimbledon was the first move in Ceawlin's successful bid for the overlordship of Britain. Three years later his uncle Cuthwulf smashed the civitas of the Catuvellauni at the Battle of Bedcanford (usually identified as Bedford). Ceawlin himself then defeated the Dobunni at Dyrham. In both cases several towns and fortresses were annexed by Ceawlin. The culmination of his career came at Fethanleag (now Stone Lyne in Oxfordshire) in 584. Whom he defeated here is not clear, but it may have been an alliance of other rulers for after this date Ceawlin was acknowledged as overlord by all rulers at least as far north as the Humber, and possibly up to Hadrian's Wall. His career ultimately ended in failure for in 592 he was ousted from power by a coup organised by his cousin Ceol.

Athelbert got back to Kent alive. It has been surmised that it was this battle that pushed the border of Kent eastward to where it lies today. Certainly this is the only known major defeat of Kent before more reliable records began to be kept, so it would make sense if this were the one that led to the territorial loss.

Athelbert was chastened by his defeat, but did not give up his ambitions. He turned across the Channel to strengthen his ties to more powerful neighbours. In about 580 he married Bertha, daughter of Charibert, King of the Franks. At this date the Franks ruled most of modern France, Belgium and the Netherlands plus a fair area of northern Germany. They were useful allies to have, though they may have regarded Athelbert as a mere minor hanger on.

Athelbert certainly gained wealth and prestige from his marriage. Cross-channel trade may have increased and he had access to military advice and aid for this future adventures. His chance came in 592 when Ceawlin lost his throne. Athelbert moved rapidly to impose his overlordship across

Britain up to the Humber. Five years later he welcomed Christian missionaries from Rome. This began the conversion of pagan England to Christianity. Although the process would take many decades to complete it brought increased prestige to Kent and to Athelbert's descendants.

Ceawlin's military career saw him fight the Dubonni at Barbury when a young man. After defeating Kent at Wimbledon he returned to crush the Dobunni at Dyrham, capturing Bath, Cirencester and Gloucester. He then defeated the Catuvellauni at Fethanleag and Bedford, capturing Limbury, Aylesbury, Benson and Eynesham. He thus became overlord of all southern Britain. He was defeated in a civil war at Woden's Barrow and retired to found a monastery in northern Wales.

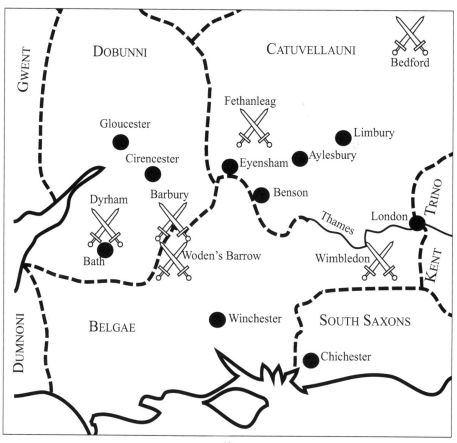

At some point in these decades a sudden and massive change came over Britain. The post-Roman civitates were swept away in a welter of bloodshed and replaced by English kingdoms. The change seems to have been very sudden and took place sometime between 550 and 590. It may have taken decades to complete, or it may have occurred in a single year. We do not know. What is certain is that across nearly all of lowland Britain the Romano-British rulers were removed and English kings took their place. In most areas the influx of English settlers combined with the impact of the political change was enough to transform the society utterly. British languages were replaced by English, Christianity by paganism and a Roman view of the world by a barbarian one. How and why this happened is uncertain, but it created the England we know today.

The statue of Queen Bertha that stands outside St Augustine's Abbey in Canterbury. The decision of King Athelbert of Kent to seek a Frankish alliance and marry a Frankish princess was to have profound long term effects on Britain. Bertha brought a Christian bishop to Canterbury to act as her personal chaplain and was instrumental in encouraging St Augustine to come to Britain from Rome and thus to start the conversion to Christianity of the pagan English.

CHAPTER 6
A NOTE ON DATES,
PLACENAMES AND SOURCES

It is fair to point out that not everyone is agreed that the climactic battle was fought at Wimbledon. The only document that names the battle calls it "Wibbandun", which is usually translated to mean "Wibba's Hill" or perhaps more accurately "Wibba's Hillock". For many years it was assumed that this meant Wimbledon, both because the names are so similar and because the location fitted other elements of the battle. Some historians have recently suggested that the place meant was Worplesdon, a village just north of Guildford. But Worplesdon is not on a Roman road, not near a river crossing and not close to boundaries between civitates, while Wimbledon is all three.

More recently the fashion among historians dealing with the Dark Ages is to discount everything for which there is no firm evidence. Those following this trend say that it is impossible to be certain where the battle took place, and so state firmly that it did not take place at Wimbledon.

The evidence is, indeed, uncertain but in my view it is persuasive. It is firmly recorded that Ceawlin and his men chased the defeated Kent army back to the Kent border. Given the usual practices of the time that means that the battle took place close to the western border of Kent - probably no more than 10 miles away. Since the Kingdom of Sussex was not involved, this would put the battle somewhere in what is now Surrey and Wimbledon is in about the right place. Moreover the location fits what we know of the geo-political situation as a battle here could have been fought for control of London, and more immediately for the crossing point over the River Wandle.

As for place name evidence, the earliest version of the name Wimbledon that we have is "Wimbedoun". For years it was assumed that this derived

45

from "Wibbandun" or "Wibba's Hill". Recently it has been suggested that the m should be given precedence over the b, making the original version of the name "Wimandun" or "Wimman's Hill". Why this version should be preferred is not entirely clear and the putative Wimman seems to have no other evidence supporting his existence, while we know that Wibba's Hill was a real place.

On balance it seems to the present writer that it is more likely than not that the battle took place at Wimbledon.

The sources for the events described here are varied, complex and open to much debate. The only source that mentions the battle itself is the Anglo-Saxon Chronicle. This was written in the 890s at the command of King Alfred the Great, King of Wessex who came from the same dynasty as Ceawlin. The effort to write a definitive history of England came in the wake of the destruction caused by the Viking wars. Alfred's scholars combed England for old books and compiled the Anglo-Saxon Chronicle from those older histories.

Although the Chronicle is a prime historical source and is generally reckoned to be accurate there are some problems with it. For events between about 650 and 790 it is held to be reliable, but before that date it is not really clear on what evidence the Chronicle relied. Perhaps there were books surviving from that early date, perhaps there were not. Perhaps the old books were inaccurate copies made in the 7th century of older books that were falling to pieces.

Perhaps the evidence came from oral legends or epic poems that no longer survive. We simply don't know. It is generally thought that the Anglo-Saxon Chronicle presents a roughly accurate version of events, but that the dates may be out by as much as 20 years or more. It is also accepted that the Anglo-Saxon Chronicle is biased in favour of Alfred's dynastic ancestors - anything less would not have been very tactful considering who was paying the bills.

Even with these admitted problems, it can be accepted that a battle was fought between Ceawlin and Athelbert and that Ceawlin won a decisive victory.

The subsequent careers of both Ceawlin and Athelbert are known from other sources. As the first English king to convert to Christianity, Athelbert had a special place in the minds of the Christian missionaries. They wrote about him and his career extensively, though they tactfully failed to mention his early defeat at Wimbledon.

Ceawlin is known mostly from the Anglo-Saxon Chronicle, but he too had a place in ecclesiastical history. Some decades after his victory at Wimbledon Ceawlin was ousted from power by a coup organised by his cousin Ceol. He then took the traditional route for an ex-ruler and became a monk. He travelled to north Wales, the native home of his grandmother, and was given some land by the ruler there who was presumably a relative of some kind. He built a church that in Welsh was dubbed "Llanceawlin", meaning "Church of Ceawlin". It is now known as Llangollen and his tomb survives.

Some centuries later a Welsh monk wrote a biography of the founder of Llangollen. We do not know how accurate this book might be in detail, though the broad outline of events does not seem unreasonable. It is from this book that most of the details of Ceawlin's life given here are taken. It must be admitted that not every scholar accepts that the Ceawlin who founded Llangollen is the same Ceawlin as he that fought at Wimbledon. Again, however, the present writer thinks that on the balance of probabilities it is likely. That there should have been two rich noblemen of the same name among the Belgae at the same time is surely not credible.

As with all Dark Age written sources, the writings about Ceawlin and Athelbert were put down many years later and we have only copies, not the originals. There has been plenty of scope for mistakes to enter the texts, and that is assuming they were accurate to start with. More likely they put down a version of the truth pleasing to the dynasty that commissioned them - much as a government press release today reflects the facts favourable to the government and ignores those of less benefit. This is not to say that the press release, or the Dark Age documents, are wrong only that they do not tell the entire story.

A key problem regarding the Battle of Wimbledon is the date it took place. The Anglo-Saxon Chronicle puts it firmly in the year 568, but as we have seen the Chronicle for these early times is not entirely trustworthy on dates. A case could be made for viewing the Chronicle dates as being about 20 years too early, so the battle may have taken place as late as 588. The later biography of Ceawlin written in Wales is no help as it mentions very few dates.

The sources for Athelbert are just as vague. We know that he died in 616, but cannot be certain when he became King of Kent. Our best source is Bede, an English monk writing in the 730s. He says Athelbert ruled for 56 years, making him King of Kent from 560 onwards. On the other hand the birth dates for his children seem to indicate that he did not marry until the 580s, and given the uncertainties of life it was very unusual for a ruler not to marry as young as possible to beget an heir. Some historians have suggested that Bede meant that Athelbert lived for 56 years, giving his birth date as 560 and his accession to the throne in about 580. This would make better sense if the Anglo-Saxon Chronicle is adjusted to put the Battle of Wimbledon in about 580. But this would involve disbelieving both Bede and the men who compiled the Chronicle. Both lived much closer to Ceawlin's time than we do and both had access to documents and oral history now lost. Perhaps they knew what they were talking about.

The Battle of Wimbledon, as with so much else in this period of English history, is something of an enigma.

ALSO AVAILABLE IN THIS SERIES